ICONIC NATIONAL PARKS

GRAND CANYON NATIONAL PARK

BY HEATHER C. HUDAK

Core Library

An Imprint of Abdo Publishing
abdobooks.com

Cover image: The Grand Canyon is the third-deepest canyon in the United States.

abdobooks.com

Published by Abdo Publishing, a division of ABDO, PO Box 398166, Minneapolis, Minnesota 55439.

Printed in the United States of America, North Mankato, Minnesota.
052025
092025

Cover Photo: Shutterstock Images
Interior Photos: Patrick J. Endres/Corbis Documentary/Getty Images, 4–5; Jonathan Dakin/500px/Getty Images, 6, 45; Red Line Editorial, 8; Shahriar Erfanian/41 Stories Photography/Moment/Getty Images, 10–11; Shutterstock Images, 12, 23, 43 (top); Steve Bly/Alamy, 15; Moritz Wolf/imageBROKER/Getty Images, 18–19; Billy McDonald/Shutterstock Images, 21; Georgi Baird/Shutterstock Images, 25; Rinus Baak/Dreamstime, 26; Bill Gorum/Alamy, 27; Brenda Fitz/Shutterstock Images, 28–29; Jim Mallouk/Shutterstock Images, 31; Ron S. Buskirk/Alamy, 34–35; National Park Service, 37; Ralph Lauer/ZUMA Wire/ZUMA Press, Inc./Alamy Live News/ Alamy, 38; Helen H. Richardson/Denver Post/Getty Images, 39; Steven Love/robertharding/Collection Mix: Subjects/Getty Images, 42 (top); Brandon Rosenblum/Moment/Getty Images, 42 (middle); Michael Quinn/ National Park Service, 42 (bottom); Craig Zerbe/Shutterstock Images, 43 (middle); Francesco Riccardo Iacomino/Moment/Getty Images, 43 (bottom)

Editor: Christa Kelly
Series Designer: Marley Richmond

Library of Congress Control Number: 2024948966

Publishers Cataloging-in-Publication Data

Names: Hudak, Heather C., author.
Title: Grand Canyon National Park / by Heather C. Hudak
Description: Minneapolis, Minnesota: Abdo Publishing, 2026 | Series: Iconic national parks | Includes online resources and index.
Identifiers: ISBN 9781098297169 (lib. bdg.) | ISBN 9798384919681 (ebook)
Subjects: LCSH: Grand Canyon National Park (Ariz.)--Juvenile literature. | Canyons--Juvenile literature. | Natural monuments--Juvenile literature. | Scenic landscapes--Juvenile literature. | National parks and reserves--Juvenile literature.
Classification: DDC 979.1--dc23

CONTENTS

CHAPTER ONE

HIKING THE CANYON

For as long as Trish could remember, her mother had wanted to hike in the Grand Canyon. Her dream was finally coming true. At dawn, Trish and her mom boarded a shuttle and headed to the South Kaibab trailhead. They planned to hike from one rim of the Grand Canyon, down to the bottom, and up to the other side in a single day. This meant they had to start early.

The sky was dark, and the morning air was cool, but Trish and her mom were prepared

South Kaibab Trail offers beautiful views deep into the Grand Canyon.

The hike from the South Kaibab trailhead to Ooh Aah Point and back is about 1.8 miles (2.9 km). It's a good hike for beginners.

with headlamps and warm clothes. After about an hour of hiking and many tight switchbacks, they reached the first marked viewpoint on the trail, Ooh Aah Point. Trish's breath caught as she watched the sunrise with her mother. The view was like nothing she'd seen before.

While South Kaibab Trail was well maintained, it was still a difficult descent into the canyon. Every part of Trish's body ached, but she kept going. By the time they reached the canyon floor, Trish was drenched in sweat. She peeled off a few layers of clothing before beginning the ascent up Bright Angel Trail.

Trish knew the climb up would take twice as long and require more effort, but the views on Bright Angel Trail made it worthwhile. After 13 hours, Trish and her mom had completed their 18-mile (29 km) trek. Trish was exhausted, but it was worth it to know she'd made her mother's dream come true.

NATIONAL PARKS

Each year, more than four million people visit Grand Canyon National Park in northwestern Arizona. A national park is an area set aside by the US government to protect the plants, animals, and natural landscapes for

FOUR RIMS

The Grand Canyon has four rims. Two are within Grand Canyon National Park. The South Rim is the most popular, with many hotels, restaurants, and activities for tourists. The area is known for its spectacular views of the Colorado River. The North Rim gets only about 10 percent of the number of tourists as the South Rim. It is much higher than the South Rim. It takes about five hours to drive from the South Rim to the North Rim.

GRAND CANYON NATIONAL PARK

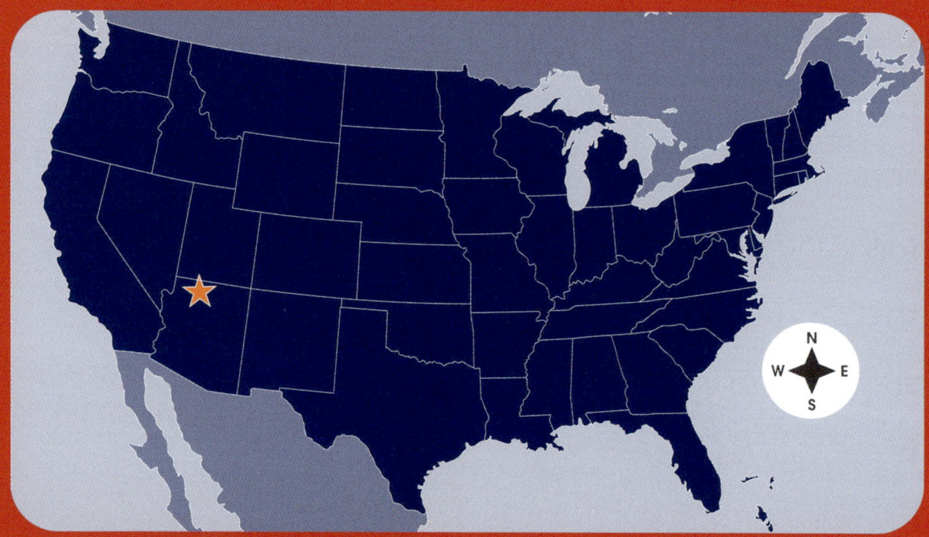

Grand Canyon National Park is in the northwestern corner of Arizona in the Southwestern United States. How do you think the park's location contributes to its geological history?

future generations. National parks are maintained by the National Park Service.

Grand Canyon National Park spans 1,218,375 acres (493,059 ha), making it larger than the entire state of Rhode Island. The park's main attraction is the Grand Canyon. It is one of the largest and deepest canyons on earth, measuring more than one mile (2 km) deep and 277 miles (446 km) long.

The Grand Canyon's colorful peaks, gorges, and ravines were formed over millions of years by natural processes such as erosion. Erosion is a process in which wind, rain, ice, and other natural forces remove topsoil and rocks from the earth's surface. Much of the Grand Canyon's erosion is caused by the Colorado River. The river winds through the canyon, slowly carving away the rock and soil. Today, visitors can travel to Grand Canyon National Park to explore the region's beauty and fascinating history.

PERSPECTIVES

MYSTERIOUS TIME GAP

Each layer of rock in the Grand Canyon represents a different period in the canyon's geological history. Geologists have found rocks that formed about 1.7 billion years ago next to rocks that formed only about 500 million years ago. There are millions of years between when these layers formed, and no one knows what happened during this gap in time. Geologists have many theories. One theory is that no rocks formed over this period. Another theory is that rocks formed but then eroded.

CHAPTER TWO

HISTORY OF GRAND CANYON NATIONAL PARK

The rock walls of the Grand Canyon tell a unique story about the history of the land. The earliest rocks are found in the inner gorge at the bottom of the Grand Canyon. They formed about two billion years ago.

About five or six million years ago, the mighty Colorado River began flowing through the region. It slowly began to erode the landscape. Over millions of years, the river cut

The different minerals in the Grand Canyon's rocks give the canyon's walls colorful stripes.

CARVING A CANYON

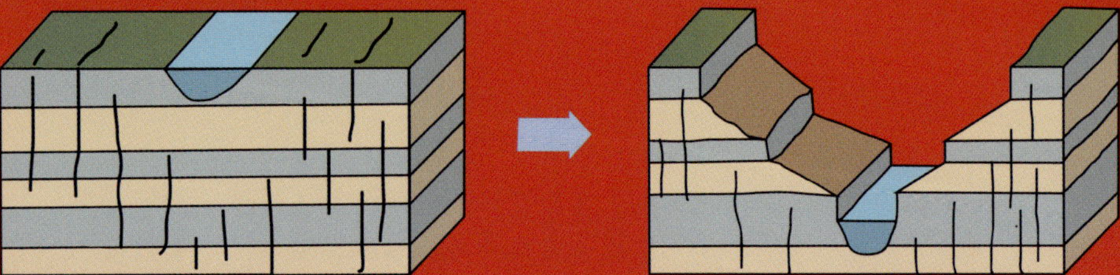

Canyons are formed when rock is eroded by natural forces. The Grand Canyon was eroded by the Colorado River over millions of years. Do you think the canyon is still being formed? Why might some rivers create canyons while others don't?

more than one mile (2 km) into the ground, bringing the canyon to its current depth.

HUMAN HISTORY

American Indians have lived in the Grand Canyon region for at least 13,000 years. Historians have documented nearly 3,400 American Indian sites from prehistoric times. They have found ancient pottery, rock art, stone houses, tools, and other artifacts. Many present-day American Indians in the Grand Canyon descended from these ancient peoples. Eleven federally recognized American Indian nations are native to the Grand Canyon area, including the Havasupai, Hopi, Hualapai, Navajo, Paiute, and Zuni nations. They have lived on, farmed, and cared for the land for thousands of years.

In 1540, Spanish explorer Francisco Vásquez de Coronado and his army came across the Hopi nation. He sent a small group with the Hopi to locate a river that would take the Spanish to the Gulf of California. After a few weeks, the Hopi people brought the Spanish to the edge of the Grand Canyon. They saw the Colorado

PERSPECTIVES

ANCESTRAL LANDS

The Grand Canyon is very important to many American Indian nations in the region. Many people from these nations are concerned about the impact of tourism on their ancestral homelands. Jason Nez is a Navajo archaeologist who works in the park. He says, "Our Native identity is tied so much to these lands. . . . Our songs and our prayers come from these places. We go to these places for healing. There are shrines that we still visit. . . . What happens to these lands happens to us. . . . We have to take care of this place so that it can take care of us."

River below. The explorers spent three days trying to reach the river before giving up. The area remained unexplored by outsiders for another 235 years.

The Grand Canyon was a blank space on the US map until the late 1850s. The US War Department sent Lieutenant Joseph Christmas Ives to explore the region, which he deemed to be worthless. Still, the US government began to encroach on the land.

In the 1860s, the government began to remove the American Indian nations of the area from their homelands. They killed many of the American Indians. Others were forced to march thousands of miles to unfamiliar places. These forced relocations continued for decades. Few American Indians were allowed to remain in the Grand Canyon area.

In 1869, a geologist and former army major named John Wesley Powell was sent on a scientific exploration of the Colorado River through the Grand Canyon. After three months, Powell and his crew became the first explorers to travel the full length of

Despite decades of forced relocations, thousands of American Indians live in the Grand Canyon area today.

the river. Powell made a second expedition in 1871 to further study the river. Many others would follow in Powell's footsteps.

MAKING A NATIONAL PARK

By the late 1880s, many Americans were moving west. Benjamin Harrison, a senator from Indiana, had concerns about how the Grand Canyon and the land around the Colorado River would be used. He asked the US government to protect the region by making it a public park but got little support. Years later, Harrison

UNESCO WORLD HERITAGE SITE

A World Heritage site is any place the United Nations Educational, Scientific and Cultural Organization (UNESCO) deems to have outstanding cultural or natural value. The Grand Canyon was chosen as a World Heritage site because of its natural beauty, geological history, diverse ecosystems, and variety of plants and animals.

became president, and in 1893, he created the Grand Canyon Forest Reserve.

Like Harrison, President Theodore Roosevelt believed the Grand Canyon should be preserved for future generations. He made it a national monument and game reserve in 1908. Nine years later, President Woodrow Wilson established Grand Canyon National Park. Since that time, the park has gained international attention. The United Nations declared it a World Heritage site in 1979.

STRAIGHT TO THE SOURCE

Lieutenant Ives wrote about his travels in his *Report upon the Colorado River of the West; Explored in 1857 and 1858*. Ives described the Grand Canyon, saying:

> *The extent and magnitude of the system of canyons is astounding. The plateau is cut into shreds by these gigantic chasms and resembles a vast ruin. Belts of country miles in width have been swept away, leaving only isolated mountains standing in the gap. Fissures so profound that the eye cannot penetrate their depths are separated by walls whose thickness one can almost span, and slender spires that seem to be tottering upon their bases shoot up thousands of feet from the vaults below.*

Source: "Grand Canyon: Explorers." *National Park Service*, 5 Sept. 2024, nps.gov. Accessed 27 Oct. 2024.

CONSIDER YOUR AUDIENCE

Adapt this passage for a different audience, such as your family or friends. Write a blog post conveying this same information to the new audience. How does your post differ from the original text and why?

CHAPTER THREE

PLANTS AND ANIMALS

Grand Canyon National Park is largely made up of desert. The desert gets hot during the day, and because the park has low humidity, there are few clouds to block the sun. When the sun goes down, the temperature quickly cools. The park's temperatures are especially cool at higher elevations. Higher elevations are also wetter.

Though the park's desert landscape may look barren at first glance, the varying elevations and unique climate provide

The bison in Grand Canyon National Park are descended from bison brought to Arizona in 1906.

PERSPECTIVES

CLIMATE CHANGE

Human activity is causing the earth to get hotter. This is called climate change. Hotter, drier weather leads to a higher risk of wildfires at Grand Canyon National Park. Scientists are studying the effects of climate change so they can help protect the park. David Lawrence is an ecologist with the National Park Service. He says, "Climate change is happening now. We're already seeing its effects . . . and using climate projections we can see that many of these effects will continue if not increase in magnitude."

diverse habitats for many species. About 2,000 species of animals, 1,700 species of plants, and a few hundred species of fungi and lichens make their homes in Grand Canyon National Park.

THE GRAND CANYON'S ECOSYSTEMS

Grand Canyon National Park is separated into five main ecosystems. Different ecosystems appear at different places in the park. Many appear only at certain elevations. Each ecosystem has a distinct mix of plant and animal species.

American Indians harvest nuts from pinyon pine trees.

The Grand Canyon's lowest ecosystem is the desert scrub. This ecosystem is found at elevations of 1,500 to 4,500 feet (460–1,400 m) above sea level. It makes up the hottest, driest parts of the park. Most water evaporates from the park before reaching this ecosystem. The majority of the plants that can survive at this elevation are small, such as cacti, sage, and yucca.

The pinyon–juniper woodland ecosystem is found at elevations of about 4,000 to 7,300 feet (1,200–2,200 m). This hot, sunny area gets little rain, but its plants have adapted to withstand the dry conditions. Utah juniper and pinyon pine trees are common in this area.

They don't grow taller than 20 feet (6 m), and their needles are designed to capture and hold water.

The ponderosa pine forest is found at elevations of about 6,500 to 8,200 feet (2,000–2,500 m). This ecosystem gets a lot of rain and snow each year. Lupines and tall pines are common here. The pines are often struck by lightning, leading to natural forest fires.

The mixed conifer forest ecosystem is found at the highest points of the Grand Canyon, from about 8,200 to 9,200 feet (2,500–2,800 m). This area gets up to 11 feet (3.4 m) of snow annually. The many deciduous trees, which lose their leaves each year, and evergreens help shelter wildlife from harsh weather.

Riparian ecosystems are not connected to elevation. These ecosystems are found along the banks of rivers and streams throughout the park. This is the smallest but most diverse of the park's ecosystems, as there is plenty of water for vegetation. Cottonwood trees, stream orchids, tamarisk, arrowweed, and redbud trees can be found in these ecosystems.

Riparian ecosystems can be found along the banks of the Colorado River at the bottom of the Grand Canyon.

ANIMALS OF THE GRAND CANYON

The Grand Canyon's diverse ecosystems support many unique species of animals. Invertebrates are the largest animal group in the park with more than 1,400 species. These animals include scorpions, butterflies, beetles, and spiders. Though small in size, invertebrates play important roles in the park's ecosystems. These animals pollinate plants, break down dead plant and animal matter, and serve as prey for other species.

Grand Canyon National Park is also home to a large number of bird species. The park's cliffs, forests, and wetlands provide nesting and foraging grounds

MANAGING THE BISON

Park rangers are working to maintain a healthy bison population in the park. The park's bison live on the Kaibab Plateau on the North Rim. There is room for about 200 bison in the area, but the herd has about 600 animals. The large numbers of bison are starting to damage the environment. They compact the soil, contaminate water, and damage habitats used by other animals. Wildlife rangers have started to move some of the bison to land owned by American Indian nations. This is decreasing the herd's population to a more manageable amount, keeping the park's ecosystems healthy.

for about 450 species of birds. Lucky park visitors may see California condors, peregrine falcons, and golden eagles soaring overhead. Great blue herons and belted kingfishers can be found in the park's riparian zones. Other common birds include canyon wrens, yellow warblers, ravens, and jays.

More than 90 species of mammals live in the park. Hooved animals in the park include elk, mule deer, and bighorn sheep. The park is also home to many

In the 1990s, California condors were on the brink of extinction. Today, nearly a hundred fly free in Grand Canyon National Park.

predators, such as coyotes, kit foxes, badgers, and mountain lions. However, many of these animals are hard to spot. Some, such as ringtails and kangaroo rats, sleep during the hot day and come out at night when the temperature cools. Others, such as bison, live only in a small portion of the park.

Some of the mammals in Grand Canyon National Park are endemic to the region. This means they are found nowhere else in the world. Among the park's

Kaibab squirrels live in the Grand Canyon's ponderosa pine forests.

endemic mammals is the Kaibab squirrel, one of the rarest animals in the United States' national parks. Also endemic to the region is the Navajo Mexican vole.

Nearly 60 reptile and amphibian species can be found throughout the park. These animals include the Gila monster, the red-spotted toad, and the canyon tree frog. One of the park's reptiles, the Grand Canyon rattlesnake, is endemic to the region.

Grand Canyon rattlesnakes eat rodents and lizards.

Many fish can be found in the Colorado River basin. Six are endemic to the area. The basin's endemic species include the humpback chub and the razorback sucker. Both are endangered.

FURTHER EVIDENCE

Chapter Three explores the plants and animals that live in Grand Canyon National Park. What is the main point of this chapter? What key evidence supports this point? Read about the park's wildlife at the website below. Does the information on the website support the main point of the chapter? Does it present new evidence?

WILDLIFE

abdocorelibrary.com/grand-canyon-national-park

CHAPTER FOUR

RECREATION

Grand Canyon National Park is one of the most popular attractions in the United States. It is the second-most visited national park in the United States after Great Smoky Mountains National Park. There are many ways for visitors to enjoy their time in the park.

Many people start their visits at Grand Canyon Village on the South Rim. This village is the most visited part of the Grand Canyon. The village is packed with hotels, restaurants,

Since its creation, more than 240 million people have visited Grand Canyon National Park.

DESERT VIEW WATCHTOWER

Desert View Watchtower is a 70-foot (21 m) stone tower on the South Rim. The tower was built in 1932 by architect Mary Colter. Its design was inspired by the architecture of the Ancestral Pueblo people of the Colorado Plateau. Today, the tower is a National Historic Landmark and a great place to look out onto the canyon. The watchtower offers 360-degree views of the Painted Desert, the Colorado River, and the North Rim. On a clear day, visitors can see more than 100 miles (160 km) into the distance.

and museums. Tourists can find information about the park's many features at Verkamp's Visitor Center in the village's historic district. The visitor center also offers shuttles to other parts of the park.

Tourists can learn about the region's history at the village's many National Historic Landmarks. These are areas preserved for their historic value. Historic landmarks in the village include the El Tovar Hotel, the Buckey O'Neill Cabin, the Hopi House, and the Grand Canyon Railway Depot.

Some rafting trips travel hundreds of miles down the Colorado River.

EXPLORING THE CANYON

There are many ways to explore Grand Canyon National Park. Those looking for an adventure can go white water rafting. Many people consider the powerful Colorado River one of the best places to white water raft in the country. Local companies offer rafting tours that last anywhere from one day to several weeks.

PERSPECTIVES

PREVENTING LIGHT POLLUTION

Grand Canyon National Park is one of the best places in the world for stargazing because the sky is so clear and dark. However, the park's skies weren't always so lovely. Until the mid-2010s, thousands of light fixtures created so much light that it was hard to see the stars. In 2016, the National Park Service began changing the park's lighting to minimize light pollution. The International Dark Sky Association declared Grand Canyon National Park a Dark Sky Park in 2019.

Another popular way to explore the area is by train. For more than 100 years, tourists have been coming to the region to board the Grand Canyon Railway. The vintage railway provides passengers with a scenic tour of the canyon and the surrounding area.

Other guests explore the canyon on mule rides. Since the late 1800s, mules have been used to carry park visitors to the depths of the canyon. Some rides last just a few hours, while others can take days.

With more than 595 miles (958 km) of trails throughout the park, there are opportunities for all levels of hikers. Bright Angel Trail is the most popular rim-to-river route in the park. The route is about nine miles (14 km) round trip and can be done in a day.

Other areas in the park can be accessed only by car. Toroweap Overlook is one such area. It is located in a remote part of the park on the North Rim. However, it is one of the most scenic viewpoints on the rim. Those who make the long trip to the overlook are rewarded with stunning views of the Colorado River, volcanic ash mounds, lava flows, and sheer cliffs.

EXPLORE ONLINE

Chapter Four talks about the different ways to explore Grand Canyon National Park. The article on the website below goes into more depth on hiking in the park. Does the article answer any of the questions you had about the park's trails?

DAY HIKING

abdocorelibrary.com/grand-canyon-national-park

CHAPTER FIVE

CARING FOR THE PARK

Each year, Grand Canyon National Park faces threats that put its landscapes and wildlife at risk. Some of these threats are natural. Natural threats include forest fires, droughts, and floods. Though these threats can devastate plants and animals, they are normal parts of life in the Grand Canyon. These natural forces help keep the landscape healthy by clearing out old, weak plants that compete for resources with newer plants.

Hundreds of people work in Grand Canyon National Park to maintain trails, educate visitors, and protect wildlife.

PERSPECTIVES

VANISHING TREASURES PROGRAM

In 1998, Congress started the Vanishing Treasures Program to help preserve architectural remains in national parks. At Grand Canyon National Park, these remains include prehistoric trail systems, ancient homes, historic mine sites, and more. According to Donelle Huffer, the Vanishing Treasures archaeologist at Grand Canyon National Park, "By preserving archeological resources . . . we provide an opportunity for present and future generations to appreciate the history of native peoples at Grand Canyon National Park."

In the past, park rangers fought against many of these natural events. For example, firefighters worked quickly to put out all fires in the park, even those caused by natural lightning strikes. This led to a buildup of dead trees and plant matter, which prevented new plants from growing. It also made fires more dangerous, as the plant matter provided more fuel. Today, the workers at Grand Canyon National Park allow natural fires to burn as long as they don't threaten human life

Fires intentionally set by park staff are called prescribed burns. These fires get rid of plant waste that could lead to big, uncontrolled fires.

and property. They even start small, controlled fires to help clear plant waste.

INVASIVE SPECIES

Some threats facing Grand Canyon National Park are not natural. They are caused by humans. One such threat is the introduction of invasive species. These are species that are not native to an area and cause harm to their new environment. Invasive species can compete with native species for resources, such as food and habitats.

Tamarisk trees grow in the Grand Canyon's riparian ecosystems. These plants take resources from native plants.

There are about 170 non-native plant species in Grand Canyon National Park. About 60 pose a risk to the park's plants, animals, and ecosystems. One such invasive plant is the tamarisk tree. Tamarisk trees spread to the Grand Canyon area in the late 1920s. Today, they are some of the most common trees in the park. To control the spread of tamarisk trees, park staff and volunteers use herbicides and handsaws. They also pull

Park rangers are tracking native fish populations in the Colorado River. The data they collect helps them learn how to protect native fish.

seedlings whenever possible. Visitors can help limit the spread of invasive species by telling staff about any non-native species they observe in the park.

WILDLIFE PROGRAMS

Rangers at Grand Canyon National Park are working hard to protect the region's native species. One way rangers protect the park's species is through wildlife programs. These programs focus on protecting endangered animals and maintaining healthy ecosystems across the park.

One of the park's current programs involves restoring the Grand Canyon's native fish species. At one

LEAVE NO TRACE

Visitors can help protect Grand Canyon National Park by leaving no evidence that they were there. Park rangers list several ways that visitors can strive to leave no trace. Visitors should avoid leaving anything in the park. They should leave plants, rocks, and historical objects alone. Tourists should respect the wildlife. They should never approach or feed animals. Campfires should be kept small and contained. They should be put out completely.

time, the Colorado River was home to many native fish. Only eight of these species remain in the Grand Canyon today, with five being found in Grand Canyon National Park. The Grand Canyon's Native Fish Ecology and Conservation (NFEC) program is working to restore the Grand Canyon's native fish populations by removing invasive fish species from the park. The NFEC also monitors the status of endangered fish species and researches ways to help the species thrive. This program is one of many ways those who love the Grand Canyon are preserving the park for future generations.

STRAIGHT TO THE SOURCE

President Theodore Roosevelt visited the South Rim of the Grand Canyon for the first time in 1903 and gave a speech to a small crowd. Roosevelt said:

> *The Grand Canyon fills me with awe. It is beyond comparison—beyond description; absolutely unparalleled throughout the wide world. . . . Let this great wonder of nature remain as it now is. Do nothing to mar its grandeur, sublimity and loveliness. You cannot improve on it. But what you can do is to keep it for your children, your children's children, and all who come after you, as the one great sight which every American should see.*

Source: "Maps of Grand Canyon National Park." *Library of Congress*, n.d., loc.gov. Accessed 27 Oct. 2024.

CHANGING MINDS

Imagine you were one of the people in the crowd when Roosevelt visited the Grand Canyon. Like Roosevelt, you believe the Grand Canyon should be protected, but some people disagree. How would you try to change their minds? Make sure you explain your opinion. Include facts and details that support your reasons.

PARK LANDMARKS

Tusayan Pueblo is the remains of an American Indian village where people lived about 800 years ago. There is a walking trail around the site.

Desert View Watchtower was built in 1932. Today, visitors can climb the watchtower for beautiful views of the canyon.

Phantom Ranch is a historical lodge at the bottom of the Grand Canyon. It can be reached by hiking, rafting, or riding mules.

Bright Angel Trail is the most popular hiking trail in Grand Canyon National Park. The trail stretches from the South Rim to the Colorado River.

Point Imperial is the highest point on the Grand Canyon's rim. It has an elevation of more than 8,800 feet (2,700 m), offering beautiful views of the canyon.

Havasu Falls is a beautiful green-blue waterfall located on the Havasupai Indian Reservation. Thousands of people visit the falls each year.

STOP AND THINK

Surprise Me

Chapter Three discusses the plants, animals, and ecosystems in Grand Canyon National Park. After reading this book, what two or three facts about the park's wildlife did you find most surprising? Write a few sentences about each fact. Why did you find each fact surprising?

Dig Deeper

After reading this book, what questions do you still have about Grand Canyon National Park? With an adult's help, find a few reliable sources that can help you answer your questions. Write a paragraph about what you learned.

Say What?

Studying national parks can mean learning a lot of new vocabulary. Find five words in this book you've never heard before. Use a dictionary to find out what they mean. Then write the meanings in your own words and use each word in a new sentence.

Take a Stand

The Grand Canyon is a sacred place for many American Indians. Today, the area is visited by millions of people each year who do not have the same connection to the land. Do you think more should be done to protect the sacred places in Grand Canyon National Park and inform tourists about their importance? Or do you think the land should be available for everyone to use as they wish? Why?

GLOSSARY

chasm
a deep, narrow opening in the ground

ecosystem
a community of organisms living together and interacting

fissure
a long, thin crack in the earth

geological
related to the study of the earth and rocks

gorge
a narrow valley with steep rock walls, often with a stream

habitat
the natural home of a plant or animal

invertebrate
an animal that doesn't have a backbone

magnitude
something of great size or importance

plateau
a large area of land with a flat surface that is higher than the surrounding land

vegetation
plants found in a particular habitat

ONLINE RESOURCES

To learn more about Grand Canyon National Park, visit our free resource websites below.

Visit **abdocorelibrary.com** or scan this QR code for free Common Core resources for teachers and students, including vetted activities, multimedia, and booklinks, for deeper subject comprehension.

Visit **abdobooklinks.com** or scan this QR code for free additional online weblinks for further learning. These links are routinely monitored and updated to provide the most current information available.

LEARN MORE

Hulick, Kathryn. *Camping and Hiking Encyclopedia*. Abdo, 2024.

O'Neal, Claire, and Tammy Gagne. *Grand Canyon*. Fox Chapel, 2024.

INDEX

About the Author

Heather C. Hudak has written hundreds of kids' books on all kinds of topics. Her favorites are books about animals and exploring different parts of the world. When she's not writing, Heather enjoys traveling. She's visited more than 60 countries. One of Heather's favorite childhood memories is of the time she and her parents took a monthlong road trip that included a visit to the Grand Canyon.